Colorful insect

Butterfly color insect

Colorful insect

Camouflage color

Camouflage green, blue, yellow

Camouflage leaves wings

Four stages of life
Egg, caterpillar, pupa
And the butterfly

Mate, lay eggs and die
Butterfly cycle of life
Has few weeks of life

Metamorphosis

Beginning new part of life

A butterflies' life

No spinal column

Invertebrate animal

Lepidopteran

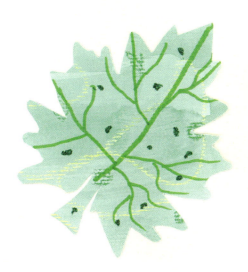

Taking off for flight

Nectar in a sunflower

Nearby some flowers

Food source from flowers

Different types of flowers

Drinking the nectar

A butterfly's wings

Gathering warmth by sunlight

Energy for flight

Two going clockwise

Purple, blue, silver colors

One counterclockwise

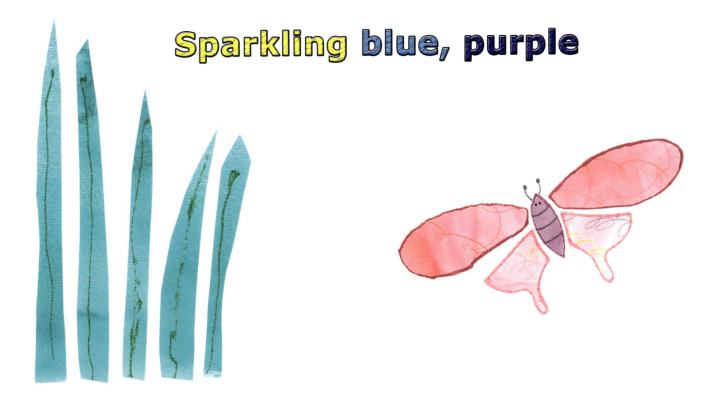

Sparkling pink, yellow

Swirling up into the sky

Sparkling blue, purple

Baby blue green wings

Zestfully playing in grass

Blue and silver sky

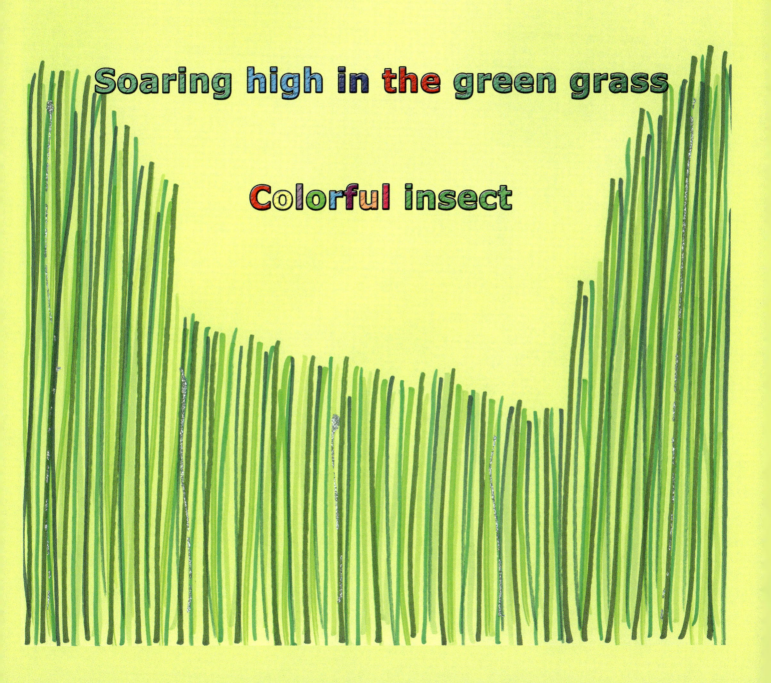

Colorful rainbow

Blue, purple, yellow, red, brown Silver, green, pink wings

Brightly colorful

Glowing rainbow in the air

Butterfly disguise

Desert rocks so hot

Images red, yellow, orange

Brown, gold, tan striped rocks

Tropical green trees

Four tiny blue butterflies

Flying toward trees

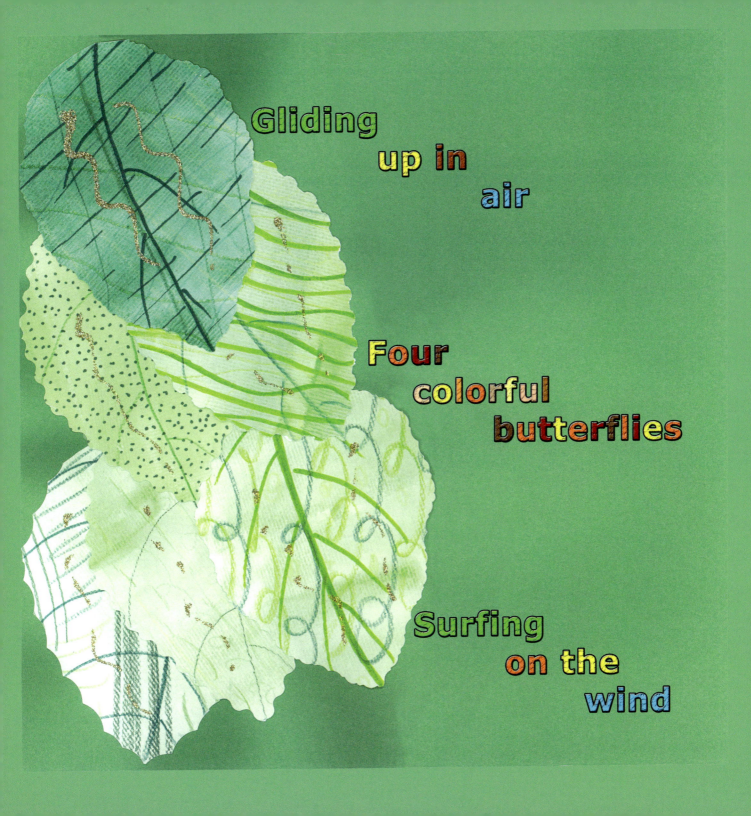

Green grass sunshine light

Yellow, blue,
purple,
green wings

Gliding over grass

About Butterflies

A butterfly's life cycle has four distinct individual phases: egg, larva, pupa (chrysalis), and adult (the butterfly). A butterfly has two forewings and two hindwings with a total of four wings. Their wings are covered with scales. They fly with their wings. A butterfly's body is divided up into three parts: the head, the thorax and the abdomen. On the head of a butterfly, it has two eyes, two antennas, and a proboscis. Butterflies drink nectar out of flowers with their proboscis which is a long tongue. Also, butterflies have six legs attached to their body (three on one side and three on the other side). There are about 15,000 to 20,000 different types of species of butterflies around the world. Many of the different species of butterflies migrate very long distances with the changing of the seasons.

Glossary

Animal: any living being that can move

Butterfly: any of numerous slender-bodied day-flying insects with large often brightly colored wings

Camouflage: the hiding or disguising of something by covering it up or changing the way it looks

Caterpillar: the long wormlike larva of a butterfly or moth

Egg: a reproductive body produced by an animal and consisting of an ovum with its food-containing and protecting envelopes and being capable of development into a new individual

Haiku: a poem written in this form: a major form of Japanese verse, written in 17 syllables divided into 3 lines of 5, 7, and 5 syllables, and employing highly evocative allusions and comparisons, often on the subject of nature or one of the seasons

Insect: any of a class of arthropods (as butterflies, true bugs, two-winged flies, bees, and grasshoppers) with the body clearly divided into a head, thorax, and abdomen, with three pairs of jointed legs, and usually with one or two pairs of wings

Invertebrate: lacking a backbone

Glossary

Lepidopteran: any of a large order of insects that include the butterflies, moths, and skippers and that as adults have four wings usually covered with minute overlapping often brightly colored scales and as larvae are caterpillars

Metamorphosis: the process of basic and usually rather sudden change in the form and habits of some animals during transformation from an immature stage (as a tadpole or a caterpillar) to an adult stage (as a frog or a butterfly)

Pupa: a stage of an insect (as a bee, moth, or beetle) having complete metamorphosis that occurs between the larva and the adult, is usually enclosed in a cocoon or case, and goes through changes inside by which structures of the larva are replaced by those of the adult

Species: a category of living things that ranks below a genus, is made up of related individuals able to produce fertile offspring, and is identified by a two-part scientific name

Spinal Column: as known as the backbone; the skeleton of the trunk and tail of a vertebrate that consists of a jointed series of vertebrae enclosing and protecting the spinal cord

Zestfully: a quality that increases enjoyment

Merriam-Webster's Word Central © 2007 by Merriam-Webster, Incorporated
http://www.wordcentral.com

Dedication

For all, who need a touch of grace on their shoulders.

Acknowledgments

First of all, I gracefully thank my parents Susan and William Fourgerel for supporting me on all of my dreams and goals that I set forth to achieve. A special thanks to my mother on all her help with this book. It would not have been possible to have this book digitally made so quickly. In addition, I extend my heartfelt thanks to my family and friends who assisted and guided me through this writing process.

Inspiration

While I was a Paraprofessional Aid at a New Jersey Elementary school, I was fortunate enough to be reintroduced to the wonderful world of children's books. This led me to believe that it would be possible for me to write my own children's book just like Eric Carle, Leo Lionni, Jan Brett and so many others. My journey began and before I knew it I was developing my book with my very own words and drawings.

I was always inspired by butterflies and their beauty. I decided that this would be my first book using colors of the rainbows and flowers to take flight.

To give poetic justice, I utilized the process of Haiku to tell the story of my illustrations. Haiku took me back in time where I enjoyed reading and creating poetry. The combination of form, content and language in a Haiku allowed me to express my thoughts in a meaningful and compact way.

About the Author

Jacquelyn received her Bachelor of Science degree in Psychology in 2004 from the University of Massachusetts, Amherst. She also received her Master of Science: Childhood Education and Childhood Special Education grades 1-6 in 2009 from Long Island University, Rockland Graduate Campus.

Jacquelyn loves to learn. She said, "I will spend my whole life learning about anything that inspires me." She loves to write, draw, read lots of books, photograph the world around her, and spend as much time with her family and close friends as possible.

Jacquelyn's favorite thing to do is, "There is nothing like cozying up next to a warm fireplace in my living room with a book in one hand and a notebook and pen in the other hand... with a cup of tea, of course."

Contact: jfourgerel@gmail.com

Butterfly Haiku
by *Jacquelyn Jaie Fourgerel*

Copyright: 2012 Jacquelyn Jaie Fourgerel **All Rights Reserved**.

ISBN-13: *978-1478362074 (CreateSpace-Assigned)*

ISBN-10: *1478362073*

Library of Congress Control Number: *2012914258*

No part of this book may be reproduced, stored in a retrieval system, or transmitted by any means without the written permission of the author.

Printed by: *CreateSpace an Amazon Company 2012*

Contact: *jfourgerel@gmail.com*

Website: *jacquelynjaiefourgerel.com*

Cover and title page designed by: *Susan Fourgerel*

Made in the USA
Middletown, DE
04 October 2024